A Breeze You Whisper

A Breeze You Whisper

Kathryn MacDonald

Hidden Brook Press

First Edition

Hidden Brook Press
www.HiddenBrookPress.com
writers@HiddenBrookPress.com

Copyright © 2011 Hidden Brook Press
Copyright © 2011 Kathryn MacDonald

All rights for poems revert to the author. All rights for book, layout and design remain with Hidden Brook Press. No part of this book may be reproduced except by a reviewer who may quote brief passages in a review. The use of any part of this publication reproduced, transmitted in any form or by any means, electronic, mechanical, photocopied, recorded or otherwise stored in a retrieval system without prior written consent of the publisher is an infringement of the copyright law.

A Breeze You Whisper
by Kathryn MacDonald

Editor – R.D. Roy
Author Photo – Judith Versavel
Cover Photo and Text Drawings – Kathryn MacDonald
Cover Design – Richard M. Grove
Layout and Design – Richard M. Grove

Typeset in Garamond
Printed and bound in USA

Library and Archives Canada Cataloguing in Publication

MacDonald, Kathryn, 1942-
    A breeze you whisper / Kathryn MacDonald.

Poems.
ISBN 978-1-897475-66-9

    I. Title.

PS8625.D638B74 2011   C811'.6   C2011-902064-5

what is the difference
between the light and the darkness
— Liu Xiaobo

Table of Contents

EAST

A Breeze You Whisper – *p. 3*
Blueberry Picking – *p. 4*
Grandchild – *p. 5*
Rehearsal – *p. 6*
One Woman – *p. 8*
Across Generations – *p. 9*
Identity – *p. 10*
Round – *p. 11*
Gatherers – *p. 12*
Avatar – *p. 13*
The Visit – *p. 14*
Afternoon Tea – *p. 16*
Strawberry Season – *p. 17*
Without a Minute Hand – *p. 26*

SOUTH

Seeds – *p. 31*
And Pregnant with Spring – *p. 32*
From My Kitchen Window – *p. 34*
Breath of Wind – *p. 35*
Gardening – *p. 36*
Spinning – *p. 37*
Like a Spark – *p. 39*
Reciprocity – *p. 40*
Spring and Other Seasons – *p. 41*
Late June – *p. 42*
Do You Remember? – *p. 43*
Earth – *p. 45*
Sudden Summer Storm – *p. 46*
Rainbow – *p. 47*

Hips – *p. 48*
The Planting – *p. 49*
Fall – *p. 51*
Fire – *p. 52*
Wind's Breath – *p. 53*
Tears and Raindrops Mingle – *p. 54*
Windigo Wind – *p. 55*

WEST

Rain and You – *p. 59*
Zen Drawing – *p. 61*
You Could Fall – *p. 62*
Flying in Light – *p. 63*
Raspberries – *p. 64*
Pleasure – *p. 65*
You and Me – *p. 66*
Apple Picking – *p. 67*
Winter Storm – *p. 70*
Cattle Sale – *p. 71*
Lines – *p. 73*
Loss Suite – *p. 74*
Abandon – *p. 76*
Falling Through Time – *p. 77*
Surreal Days – *p. 78*
Winter Solstice – *p. 79*
Tomorrow – *p. 80*
Nine Months – *p. 81*
Yesterday – *p. 82*
Kneading – *p. 84*
Other – *p. 85*
Gathering Lilacs – *p. 86*

NORTH

After Dark – *p. 91*
Touchstone – *p. 93*
Sandcastles No Longer Occupy My Hands – *p. 94*
Seeing – *p. 95*
Spiritland – *p. 96*
Sea Song – *p. 98*
Amulet Woman – *p. 100*
Reading Gwendolyn MacEwan – *p. 101*
May Day – *p. 102*
Landscape – *p. 103*

ABOVE & BELOW

Migration – *p. 109*
Mythic Alchemy – *p. 110*
Star Shower – *p. 114*
Ordinance – *p. 115*
Gifts – *p. 116*
On the Other Side of Sunrise – *p. 117*
Light Quest – *p. 118*
Dragon Lair – *p. 120*
Hitchhiker – *p. 122*
City Hunter – *p. 123*
After the Accident – *p. 124*
Friendship – *p. 125*

Acknowledgements – *p. 126*
Notes – *p. 127*

EAST

Last autumn's chastened berries still on one tree,
Spring blossoms tender, hopeful, on another.
— Jane Hirshfield

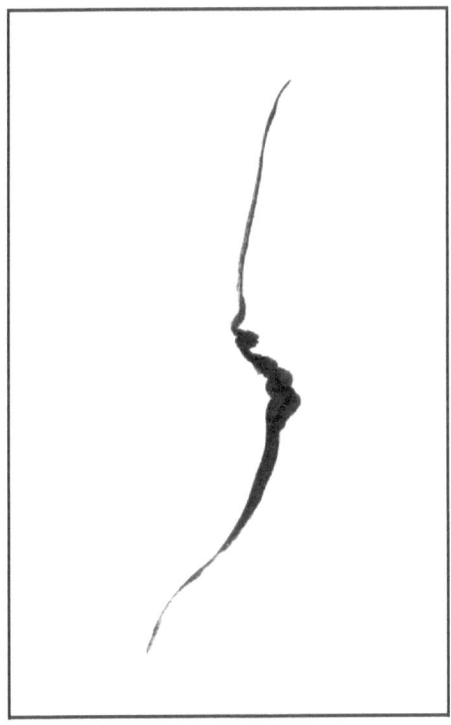

A Breeze You Whisper

A breeze, you whisper.
A bird, you soar and hover
before dropping into the nest
hidden within my tossing limbs.

Blueberry Picking

My womb was full of you
the first time
I went berry picking
at Lake of the Woods,
round and placid
like the heavy rocks
from which the prickly
bushes seemed to grow.
I fondled the sweet
berries with my tongue,
staining my lips blue.
You sensed my mood
then and quieted your boxing fists.
Now your seed grows
beneath another woman's heart.

Grandchild

Unmask. Discard. Trust intuition's seed,
your heart's yearning for its truth.
Like Arthur, knight of old,
remove the sword wedged in life's
stone to free the birthing promise.
Take up the challenge of the quest.
Dig deep inside to find your magic core,
the wisdom that comes from harmony.
Grandchild, this is my wish for you:
take flight.

Rehearsal

> ...and by dance that mimed ascension...the soul
> came out of itself and flew away.
> — Eliade

The notes scale the
keyboard   tumbling
over themselves
while she sits   legs
askew   tying
pink ribbons   over
arch and ankle
muscles taut
anticipating.

Her body at the
barre   no longer
round   but
supple and firm
   responds
to the rhythm
the muscles pulling
and pushing   the
hair on her
neck wet where
it slips free.
With grace and strength
feet push against
floor in very
even time.

With head inclined
she moves in
perfect unison with
the sound   mirror-
image repeating motion.
Subtle arms sculpt
air   like a breath
her body presses
and lifts
darkens her eyes
her lips smile.
Smoothly
   she ascends
before me   her image
vanishes from the glass.

One Woman

Your laughter bubbles
rising gurgling geyser
filling me with love.
Exuberant you
living fully in today
deep in life's river
currents and rapids
moving with enthusiasm
welcoming flotsam
tossed up in turmoil
longing, needing and loving
glowing like sunrise
or polished wet stones
exploding into warm air
a surprise hug
manifesting joy
and rampant passion
all wrapped in one woman.

Across Generations

Grandma's face, burnished and worn
like walnut, graces my memories.

You remind me of her
in your earthiness,
although you lack her grey-streaked bun
and crosshatched wrinkles.
Something about your eyes,
their intensity and feeling
burrowed deep
in pain never mentioned
and joy.
You squat in your garden
fingers easing plants into soil.
Lilies and iris and leafy hosta
will reward your eyes with colour
(yellow, purple and pale-dawn blue).
Your honey-brown hair caught in a knot
strays free in a gust of spring breeze
as hers used to do.

Later you'll sit by the fire pit
legs wrapped in a quilt
sewn during snowy days
as forget-me-nots were sown today.
The cloth pieced into squares
patterns creating stories shared
from woman's heart and hand.

In her season she was like you
young and loving
and loved.
By orange embers below night's sky
time collapses into sparks
across generations.

IDENTITY

I am all the grandmothers:
French, English, Irish, and
the Wendat woman
who was born on an island in Big Marsh.

I am Sky Woman
   falling, falling into an abyss
   without knowing that I will be saved
   by muck becoming island on a turtle's back.
I am grandmother moon
   a soft and gentle light, a monthly rhythm
   a light dancing on water, shimmering on snow.
And I am the earth goddess
   mother of all.
I walk the circle of my life
   past becomes future.
I become my children
   and grandchildren.
My seeking leads me to a future I
   cannot imagine, through a past cast in shadows.
And I walk, circling as the moon circles earth,
   as earth circles sun.
This dance weaves
   life-shaping patterns
   tells my story.
            "Who are you?" someone asks.
            "I am the story of myself,"
            comes the reply.
            – so says the Kiowa poet.
I am the story of the grandmothers.
I am becoming the story of grandchildren.

Round

All the cookies of my girlhood were round,
those that Grandma made from rolled-out dough
cut with a glass and dusted with glistening sugar.
Those made by my Mom dropped with a spoon
onto the shiny cookie sheets,
raisons and nuts peaking out through the batter.
Cookies were served on round plates,
stored in round tins.
Round is the shape of my girlhood,
round as a hug.

Gatherers

Bending over berry brambles
scent rises, surrounding me
with summer's perfume,
rich and sweet.

Long ago, I followed two old women
picking wild fruit:
blackberries, red raspberries, gooseberries
along the liminal path
between the railroad track
and my father's fields.
In their garden, they gathered
red and black currents into baskets.
Summer fruits, all these,
lush and ripe with life and love.

Is it *sub*liminal yearning that has led me here
where wild berries also grow along fencerows
bordering another railroad track
that cuts through another parcel of land?
Here, wild strawberries fringe pastures
and fields of native grasses,
like waves rippling timeless shores.
Here, I am growing old,
following in the wake of ancestors.

Now, it is me tending currents and raspberries,
filling baskets, harvesting memories
as old as time, as steady as seasons
discovering thresholds of memory.

Avatar

She clasps my hand
her soul tremoring through
    fingertips
her tears creating rainbows
    of release.

She turns through her nights
courting images
and exaggerations
that revolve   like
the moon   through her
seasons and
from the pinnacle of her
rotation
she spirals   like
the dream
    shattering.

Stooping
she gathers the fragments
carefully placing them
in paint pots
later
to brush across canvas.

The Visit

"I live a very simple life,"
she said,
working her fingers against each other
like an old woman
rubbing a rippling scrub board.
Her gaze lifted
eyes seeking the dimensions of the untended garden.
"See the iris.
All the colour and texture of spring.
Promises.
Lots," or lost, I can't be sure, "of promises,"
she said.
Her voice gained strength
as she lifted herself from the slatted porch,
her body rising easily
like a downy feather
caught in a surprising breeze.
Kittens tumbled and rolled
among the grasses.

Her eyes lifted
searching beyond the fecund patch of earth
moving along the contours of the near-dry creek bed.
Like her furrowed skin
it lay exposed.
"Rain's a little late,"
she said,
as if reading my thoughts.
The pair of mallards banked in perfect unison.
"Sky dancing,"
she said.
Wisps of hair clung to her moist cheek.

"Don't like to talk about it.
No use stirring up all that stuff.
Don't want to remember.
It was a long time ago.
Not important."
But she answered my question
by letting her hand
brush quickly over mine.

Afternoon Tea

Brittle bones embrace me
as I stretch to kiss his wizened cheek.
Across the simple room
her eyes lift from the game of solitaire
and the crocheted shawl slips
from her blue-flowered lap as she stands.

"Sometimes I think we've always been cold," she says,
warming her narrow hands over the steaming tea-kettle.
I put my gifts of fruit and biscuits on the table.
Her voice softens to a whisper,
"Perhaps we've lived too long,"
and she turns her face from me.

I left him sitting in the worn wing chair
while she dealt another round of solitaire.

Strawberry Season

i

Red-ribboned braids fall
over her shoulder
refuse to stay
back.

Grandma kneels
on a skirt of yellow rose buds
grey hair pulled to a bun
straggles free of pins
brushed back
with the hand
just like the child's.

In a clay bowl
she collects strawberries.
She draws
another between her lips.

It is her birthday.

ii

In the field, earth
curls behind plough
curls black and wet.

The strap
Daddy carries is soft
and strong
and smells
of straw and horses.

She laughs
legs sticking straight out
she fingers the strip
of long hair running
before the mare's broad back
and the child is bigger
bigger than Grandpa
bigger even than Daddy

iii

The hooked door
in Granny's skinny
kitchen keeps the child
from falling
into the cellar
with carrots and
apples and glass
jars of peaches and chilli sauce

but once
she felt the cellar
dark and wet
like morning grass
her stomach filling
with knots
fearing the collapse
of the whole house
into this damp pit.

iv

By standing on tiptoes
she can just reach
the pump handle's upward thrust.
Full buckets sprinkle grass
between well and kitchen.

Mama pours into an oval
pan on the hot stove.

In the circle of heat
she watches water grow
up the tub's sides
her moving hands
making waves
becoming mermaid
but Mama doesn't
see beyond her mending basket.

v

Turkeys are everywhere
grey feathers dull
bodies too big for heads
red combs flopping
gobble, gobble, gobble.

Granny ties
one upside down
in the tree.
The child sees
blood squirt
red splattering
Granny's hand.
After a while
it just hangs limp.

She runs
toward low branches
branches good for climbing.
Today she does not climb.
Today she makes a nest
among bruised apples
grasping knees with hands
pulling them close
to her chest.
She curls into a ball.

vi

She listens to Granny's
voice in the room nearby

smells cinnamon scented tea
and smouldering leaves
floating like the fog
horns over the river
beyond the street.
She sits still
knowing there'll be ice cream
before going home.

vii

Snow overflows ditches
covers fences and the garden
path.   Pine and roasting
turkey greet her
at the open doorway. She smiles
hugs Granny and
aunts and uncles and cousins
and Grandpa will tell
stories   how he rode
a horse all the way to Niagara
and how it took four days.

Grandpa has a sword upstairs
sometimes the child holds it
but not today.

Pitchers of yellow milk
and bowls and bowls of every
good thing sit on the table.

Granny won a prize at the fair
for her Christmas pudding.

viii

The rope swing hangs
from the tree. The child
pumps her legs until
she is flying
wants to touch the sky.
She can see iris and
forsythia growing along
the shallow creek bank.

Granny sits on the step
paddling the butter
against the bowl's wooden sides.
She drinks the salty milk
sits looking past the verandah
toward the tree's webbed shadow.

ix

There is a certain place
between the iris and creek bed
where she often plays

but today she sits on the verandah
tries not to hear the adult voices
tries not to see the empty berry bowl.

Brushing hair from her eyes
she sees Granny lying still
near the open doorway.

Breathing chrysanthemums and lilacs
she touches Granny's speckled hand
and whispers Granny goodbye.

Without a Minute Hand

Mittened hands dig
tunnels in ditch banks
form icy forts
territory marked
by a circle of snow
angels

        across
muddy fields to
bush and creek
balancing the tree
trunk bridge over
tadpoles   snakes
deep run-off
fearing the fall

during dog days
we ride bikes
to the windmill
pumping cool water
over each other's
heads   climbing
the skeletal frame

with arms outstretched
we walk miles along
narrow rails   stooping
with ear against buzzing rail
whistle   black smoke
conductor and caboose man

third cutting
and the hay smells sweeter than the first
ripening corn will soon
fill the bins and pumpkins
will grin on the step
soon   my face will be
wet with new snow

SOUTH

*Mistrust no one who offers you
water from well, a songbird's feather,
something that's been mended twice.
Always travel lighter
than the heart.*

— Lorna Crozier

SEEDS

Seeds are real for this farmer's daughter
sown in fields a hundred acres wide.
Seeds are real for this Wendat granddaughter
intermingled patches of corn and squash and beans
to feed the People during the hungry season.
And still seeds are intentions planted in the imagination
to rest cocoonlike until the time is ripe for blossoms
and the slow growth toward fruitfulness.

And Pregnant with Spring

The moon rises full and pregnant with spring
up over hints of green grass and fields of hay
losing even this scant hue in the falling dusk
while up in the darkening sky
promises glow round as the seasons.

Dawn comes sooner now.
With the crossing of the vernal equinox
we slip toward earlier sunrises.
With longer days red wing blackbirds
return to the pond, even when snow lingers
on the north shore and the mallard drakes
parade themselves before the hens.
Robins sport breasts red as sunrise
and the woods shield singing goldfinch
from the harrier, red-tail hawk, and kestrel.

Our days are as long as the sun's journey
across the arc of blue sky
and we shed winter like a garter snake
slipping out of dried skin, strewing coats
and gloves and snow boots.

We yearn for the taste of Egyptian onions
that spring up through snowdrifts near the door
add their green shoots to egg salad sandwiches
eaten on the porch facing south, facing pond,
anticipate summer's heat and busier days to come:
cutting and raking and baling hay
in its turn to become winter feed but not now.
These days are gifts between shovelling and slogging.
Time to watch stillness come alive again.
Time to reawaken and shake off winter's cocoon.

The moon rises full and pregnant with spring
warm white light glowing silver with shadows
making her way from east to west
in the path set out by the blazing sun
circling earth while earth circles sun.

From My Kitchen Window

From my kitchen window I gaze across the way
my hands busy, creaming butter and eggs
while my eyes slip into a sea of pale blossoms
where only yesterday, it seems, stark branches
spread. Now blossoms scented with honey
drift on spring's breeze lightly
circle me as my arms circle the bowl
becoming as we all become in spring – something else.
Soon my vision will behold all the colours of green
rustling whispers of hope and secrets of transformation
until a pale golden glow sensuous as dawn
stirs deeply and the pears ripe and moist
taste like kisses on my lips.

Breath of Wind

Spring arrives on a breath of wind
sudden surprise to my winter-cramped soul,
compelling windows to open,
creating yearning to scuttle winter's debris.

Down by the pond mallards build their nest.
Redwing blackbirds perch stark against grey-green cattails.
Swallows dart and dive above the still water.
Downy woodpeckers' rat-tat-tat echoes my heartbeat.

My hands in the soapy bucket
move slower now than seasons' past,
wiping away the grimy residue of ice and snow,
becoming a celebration that once seemed chore.

From window to window
daydreams sweeten the air like clover,
like anise-hyssop in my teacup.

Daydream green fields and blue
forget-me-nots in the grass, violets,
periwinkle, and strawberry blossoms.
Daydream exuberance on the rampage.
Daydream rebirth.

From window to window
heart listens, soul soars,
and when sleep comes
frogs will croak all night down by the pond.

Gardening

The couple knelt
one at either edge of the garden plot
pulling the string taut between
posts that they hammered into moist black soil.

In their season
the poppies had
lifted bright orange heads
on spidery stalks
swaying in breezes
that promised hot summer days.
Now the pods hung
by a length of white thread
from the crooked
hook on the wall,
their horde of seeds
dormant, protected
by green skin and brown
fluted caps.

He removed the stalks from their place
and broke the pods into her cupped hands.
She dropped the seeds into the trough
he dug with the blade of his hoe,
placing them evenly under the string
knowing their latency would cease
with the first warmth of spring sun.
They pulled the stakes and rolled
the string into a ball once again.
He raked the earth smooth
and saw the wind blow through her hair
as she stooped to pick a dried leaf
blown from the rustling oak tree.

Spinning

Her scent scatters particles of night
seeking beneath spring's moon
what you and I might call romance
and others simply lust
or what Darwin might have called
survival of the species.

It was at dusk
after the sun had journeyed
over earth's rim
but in that short span
when a warm afterglow
drenches the garden in amber light.

We walked the path
shaded by the drooping willow
where backlit, translucent,
a luna moth of the *Saturniidae* family
hung drying its wings
preparing for flight.

You held my hand
in the silence of our breathing
as we witnessed this rare glimpse
into the otherworld of night
where dark seldom reveals
mysteries to our light-seeing eyes.

Soon Luna would sail
early summer skies, her weeklong life
begun. How short a time
to mate and seed her eggs,
before life's cycle circles
to begin anew.

We hold this moment
as the present gifts us
these wings of limy green,
and beneath the rising moon
we stand transfixed
spinning memory's cocoon.

Like a Spark

Beyond the porch where we sit sipping coffee
an oriole the colour of fire and cinders
flits from branch to branch like a spark
among spring-green leaves
calling raucously with wild abandon
to his mate (we wonder)
or maybe seeking one.
We crane our necks awkwardly
willing our eyes to see around corners
through branches and leaf cover
into the world of wings far above
where this moment is all and everything.

Reciprocity

A wren lives in a nest
across from the bittersweet.
She's protected there
in the shadow of its tangled vines.
Her world is small
confined as she is to mothering.
Around her lies the garden
where herbs and flowers grow.
Seeds and fruit abound
(not to mention crawly things
and bugs on wing).
Below her the pond gurgles
and frogs sunbathe
on a tangle of rock
so a drink and a bath
are not far away.

For my part, I plant and weed
and as I do
her song lightens my day
as much as the sun arching above
and I pause to wonder:
whose garden is it anyway?

Spring and Other Seasons

That warm afternoon
we shut the motor off
letting the boat drift
toward shore.   I
jumped into the still
cold water   pulling
hand over hand
with the lake's gentle
rhythm pulling us
far onto the bank
the glittering sand pushing
between my toes
your laughter in my ears.
We watched the rare heron
fly with her young
my back pressed into
white shells
your wind-brown body shading
my eyes from the sun.

Through my window
I watch darkness
listen for the robin's first call
the bantam crows
the guinea fowl mark
a boundary.
In the first light
I tip a small basket of shells
through my fingers   feel
each intricate form
evoke other days.
The children call.
I make my bed before
tucking a shell far
into the pocket of my jeans.

LATE JUNE

The sun struts across the long arc of sky
announcing summer's arrival, his rays kissing
the upturned faces of flowers:
yellow sundrops and fiery lilies.
He is a promiscuous lad, a charmer
his warmth as sensuous as Leonard Cohen's voice.

Do You Remember?

Do you remember
the afternoon?
We stand together
– it is 2:30 during
an impossibly hot, dry June –
looking out
from our kitchen window.

We watch a doe
– the colour of burnished copper –
slipping from tree cover to move
down, down toward the water's
edge of our pond. You comment
that she must be awfully thirsty,
coming so close to the house.

She pauses, lifting her head
toward us, as if hearing our whispers.
For a long moment we stare
across the gulf of grass and weeds
of our backyard. Then she lowers
her head, continuing down the
sloping grade to the water.

Calmly she stands – head down –
before slowly rising up the bank
and into the newly mown
field to make her way
back to the cover of bush and fence row.
We are one in our watching
under this magical enchantment.

You say that her chances are not very good,
and I question why. You say
a row of tree stands line the border
beyond the sanctuary of our fields
where hunters sit in wait
for hungry deer to leave cover and venture
into the sights of their guns.

My heart – that soared and beat quickly
at the sight of her – now moans a sigh
mourning the fleeting pond-side image
being replaced with darkly stained shadows.
Do you remember how we turned away
– our backs to the glass –
suffering a loss yet to come?

Earth

Worms wiggle through soil
and at the end of the robin's beak.

Ants build labyrinthine passageways
and a room fit for a queen's eggs.

Below the raspberries
a brown field mouse curls in her nest.

Away from the garden path
under the evergreen rabbits burrow.

My fingers reach for weedy roots
find mysteries buried deep.

Gravity holds more than loam
to its stony heart.

Sudden Summer Storm

Wind lifts the canopy overhead
flutters
settles down once more
gusts
rippling the netting in waves.
Leaves whisper as the maples toss.
We watch heavy-bottomed clouds
burst.
Sheets of grey rain rush toward us.
Suddenly the horizon seems near,
woods and fields and even the yard
swallowed
by the sudden summer storm.

Rainbow

Into the rain-drenched cup of the lily
my eyes devour the rainbow
resting there within petals star-white
and I dance within the circle
of my garden becoming spirit
soul unbound by gravity
dancing on moonbeams
among the candle's glow.

Hips

Hips –
round as a woman's
rouged cheeks –
hang
among the drying leaves
of the wild rose
growing at my garden's edge.

Above, tree-tops swirl,
wind casts – sky fishing –
while creaking branches
shed yellowing leaves.

Unseasonably hot and droughty
even for mid-August,
the garden and the woods behind
suffer
stalks and seed pods
shatter
in vanishing green.

Fall approaches too quickly
for aging bones sitting silently
for eyes watching monarchs flutter
preparing to journey
across lakes and beyond.

Dry leaves brush,
scratch, and rattle,
yearning
for drumming raindrops,
complaining in ways
spirits understand
but ignore,
while the dry wind
warms rosehips into glow.

THE PLANTING

Her grey frizzled head bent
over the browning iris spears.
Her trowel dug into the soft
earth loosening foxtails and
other wild things that she
tossed into a pile on her left.
She pulled a knife from the
pocket of her baggy green pants
and I imagined peering over her
shoulder as she sliced through
their thick tubers splitting them
like amoebae   in two. She
occasionally brushed the hair
from her eyes with the side
of her arm and her face bore
the stains of the earth.
She gradually worked her way
through the garden from east
to west as she said was her
habit.   Her face was quite
red from the sun. When her
shadow was short she moved to
the shade of a MacIntosh tree
where soon her head lolled to
one side. The mewling cry of
the heifer woke her and after
offering a bucket of water she
returned to the bed carefully
burying the roots according to
plan. She gathered the
mat she had knelt on   the
trowel and the knife   placing
them in a weathered reed basket

plucking an apple from the
tree as she passed on her way
to the shed. Later that evening
she sat in her rocker and
welcomed the frost   and
longed for the snow. In her
head danced a rainbow   a prism
of crystal.

Fall

Beneath the faded porch umbrella
we sit
the gusting breeze rippling pages
of our separate magazines
our skin still warm
from the early September sun
just falling behind the row of maples
that marks the edge of our world.

Soon dusk will settle over us,
a cool embrace
and your head will nod toward the page
your fingers relaxing
falling
pulled by earth's gravity
as the earth pulls itself
to the dark side of our day.

FIRE

I saw
the dried leaf curl
the smouldering edges
drawing together
forming a tunnel
a pungent
arc of gold.

Wind's Breath

Sparks lift on wind's breath
Scatter across a dark landscape
Like out of season Perseid showers
Stirring fear in my heart

I run through the night
Circle dove-grey ashes
Dull and dead above
Glowing and hot below

With every burst of wind
Crimson rises from ash
More and more embers
Threaten dried grass

My rake pulls ash centreward
Vainly trying to smother
Glowing remnants of afternoon
Debris deceptively buried

Whispering to wind
Begging prayers to pause
I push my helpless rake down
Revealing yet more hot coals

Wind calms mysteriously
With bucket in hand
I run back and forth
Dousing chimera

Incendiary wind
Rises once more
At my feet steaming cinders
Remain soggily earthbound

Tears and Raindrops Mingle

Tears and raindrops mingle
in the garden plot
redolent with promises
as they flow over the boundaries
of soul and cloud
to sift softly into dry earth
plumping dreams and seeds
whose sweet nectar will beckon
summer-cloaked yellow and black
bees, swallowtail butterflies
and ruby-throated hummingbirds.
Whispers buzz and whir.
Winged rituals dance labyrinthine paths
invisible to my eyes
stirring memories of mythic gardens
out of time when sky and earth
separated from swirling chaos
and eons of ice and melt
cooled volcanic fires
making way for dragons and dragonflies
making way for tears and rain.

Windigo Wind

Ice strikes windowpanes
driven by windigo wind;
wild unnatural howls
more frightening than spirit wolves,
they ride the night to my door.
I stare through icy breath crystals
cutting off moon and stars
setting me adrift below.
The drumming of my heart
quickens to match the lashing storm
paced to primal rhythm
unearthed like fear or chaos
before nature settled what would be
land, water, fire and air
before dark and light were separate beings.
I shut my eyes against the night
telling stories to remind myself
beneath this barren winterscape
life lies dreaming images of rebirth.
I burrow beneath blankets
seeking safety like other creatures
in warren, cave, and nest
to weather winter's frigid chill
by feeding my dying soul with dreams,
dried berries, and other seedy things.

WEST

It is November, and we yearn
for flight
 — Carolyn Smart

Rain and You

From under the eaves
we listened
to pounding waves beyond
rain streaked panes
jagged light
exposing
tangled limbs
wind whipped hackberry
and willow.
High
from the dormer window
we watched
Lake Erie heave and
pierce the bluff.

With rain and you
on my lips
we descended
the steep slope
toward the uprooted
willow tossed
carelessly
on the beach
and walked
with the rising
sun on our backs.

That morning
we found
a swallow colony
in the yellow
clay bluff
circles
overlooking the lake.

We entered
the water then
our clothes
with other useless things
scattered on the sand.

Zen Drawing

My pencil touches the paper
while my eyes touch your high brow
and follow the curve of your cheek
down into your course grey beard
where I become entangled
my eyes lost in your manliness
while the pencil spins a tightly woven web
before moving against the paper
upward to form your listening ear
– so soft in contrast –
before finding the firm bones of your cheek
and the shadow laying beside your nose
then along its ridge to the bridge
linking your blue eyes
eyes that see what others miss
– another's downward gaze.

You Could Fall

You could fall into me
again and again
weightless as a bird's bone
while I taste honey
pull feathers from my tongue
see us reflected in your eyes
skydancing.

Flying in Light

Mallards preen at pond
Sit together in sun
We watch from porch
Red-winged blackbirds call
Cacophony rises
Out of spring-bare woods
All about comes alive
As the first full moon of spring
Rises in the east

Raspberries

Her body leans into the row
seeking plump, ripe fruit.

Her fingers drip raspberry juice
(later she'll notice the stains).

But now she reaches between brambles
avoiding thorns under July's hot sun.

In the trees at the garden's edge
birds scold
as if none might be left for them.

Time lengthens.
She drifts along the row
slowly filling her basket.

Later, at the scarred kitchen table
she and her man will float
berries in cream.

Pleasure

Your fingers touch the buttons
pushing them through each hole
creating a V in my white nightgown.
All the while, your eyes seek mine,
hold them, as your hands reach
to caress my breasts,
and I am eager for your touch.
You pleasure me
and more.
Have done so for half my lifetime
and more.

You and Me

You and me and a yellow mustang
riding the wind.
You and me under the sun.
The two of us discovering touch,
sunshine on our faces,
fire in our souls.

So slowly we do not notice
wind settles into breeze
ruffling clover to scent the air,
cattle lowing to calves
down by the fossil ponds beyond woods.
You and me walking.

The two of us sipping coffee
late mornings by the woodstove
snow drifting across the drive
wind whistling through leaves left
clinging to the oak we planted in our yard.
Later you'll go to your shop repairing chairs
loosened by years of wiggling children
and joints grown dry with time
while I will turn to wordsmithing
memories and dreams
of you and me
with the sickle moon hanging
among stars in night's sky.

Apple Picking

His eyes as blue and clear as lake water;
his hair shimmering like the silver foam set free
by waves splashing against shore.
Her eyes the colour of earth;
her hair like the dark side of the moon.

He sits on a chair, bent over, tying work boots.
She gathers baskets – a trug and one woven of willow.
He slips on a bright, royal blue jacket,
reaches for a worn cane with a crook,
goes out to start the engine of the old pick-up truck.
She pushes her feet into running shoes
without untying laces,
pushes her arms into a faded mauve jacket,
picks up the baskets and follows him past the oak
whose leaves were green, then yellow-tinged,
now showing an orangey glow
like embers in the stove's belly.
A dying phoenix, she thinks.

They drive along the edge of the hill field
past round bales of hay stored in rows
anticipating cold winter days.
They take the bend between crimson sumacs,
follow the path behind woods they call the bird sanctuary,
head toward barnyard and cattle pasture
toward a gnarled apple tree older than time.
In the spring, blossoms blushed pink in a giant bouquet.
Now, its branches hang heavy with red balls of fruit,
each striped at the base with gold.

She steps from the cab onto the runningboard,
lifts her foot over the side and rolls up and over
onto the pick-up bed - not as graceful a manoeuvre
as once it was, but effective. She stands.
Her head rises among dipping apple branches.
He slides out of the cab, reaches for his cane,
moves to the back of the pick-up and lowers its tailgate.
"I'll pick up here," she says,
"and you can pick the lower branches."
But the boy says "No."
The man lifts one leg while the other crumbles.
He falls with a thud and an exhalation.
His cane clatters to the ground beside him.

She seems to take the length of the truck-bed in one step,
slides down over the end.
He lies flat on the ground, eyes shut.
Panic squeezes her heart with cruel fingers.
One hip seems lower than the other;
both legs lay bent at the knees.
Then he opens his eyes, raises slowly onto one elbow,
sits, then tests the strength in his legs.

The crisis past,
she steps upon a large rock
between the tree trunk and the truck,
pulls herself up once more
into the realm of branches and sky.
In one hand, they each hold a basket;
in the other, their fingers begin grasping and twisting fruit,
pulling it free of the stem,
placing it carefully - so as not to bruise.
Wind rustles the few remaining leaves,
pecking their cheeks like an angry bird.
Looking skyward she sees three children
each wearing hooded sweatshirts,
hears laughter in the breeze, blinks, and they disappear.

Three times, he moves the truck so she can reach
around the circle of outstretched branches,
growing buoyant as the baskets fill.
He plucks the tempting fruit nearer earth.
Their bodies stretch, twist, and bend
in a dance of harvest celebration.
Their mouths anticipate applesauce, apple crisp,
anticipate baked apples with cream.
She slides the heavy baskets toward the cab,
wedging them together so they won't tip,
so apples won't spill
across the rippling floor-bed as they journey back,
reversing direction along the same path.

At the house, he feeds the embers
with deadwood cut and split another day.
They hang their coats on hooks,
stashing shoes and boots beneath,
warm frozen fingers over the leaping flames.
The young woman, the boy too, have had their play.
Now the couple sit in company with love,
mellowed and grown comfortable over seasons of green,
turned to yellow, a season erupting into orange flame.
Their stiff and tired bodies ease toward sleep.

Winter Storm

she marks
distance with care
measuring her path
from fencerows
while he tugs
at her memory
        when motion was joy
        when their bodies easily
        skimmed white powder
now she
inches slowly downward
feeling sleet on her forehead
through whiteout she sees
        his blue eyes
        his hand reach
        feels it cup her small breast

Cattle Sale

Stay safe, stay safe, stay safe.
The words tumble over each other
silently in my head, like a chant,
as the tractor – and you – travel
down the road toward Marysville.

As I wash dishes, gather laundry
pick up a book for distraction
the words never cease
become meditation, breath
resonating within every pore.

You would be feeding cattle now
walking among them quietly
with your crooked barnyard cane
watching and reading contentedness
in their solid bovine bodies.

You feel no sense of worry
as I pace and fidget
listening for the John Deere's
rumble and the crunch of tires
once more in our yard.

Memories lodge in my bones
vulnerabilities of machines
striking and ending breath
of those I love – Father
and Grandson – roadway casualties.

For today, the magic works,
and you are framed in our doorway
your voice warming my heart
but when the cattle are sold, my relief
will merge with your regret.

You will miss your bovine beauties
and their tiny offspring that you
protect from coyotes and wolves
in spring, and in winter you will miss
steam rising off their warm hides

and myriad things I have no knowledge of.
We sit at either end of a child's sea-saw
as the day of the sale grows nearer,
emotions rising and falling as we
prepare for letting go and something new.

Lines

There is a line my eyes draw
where the lake meets the shore,
that liminal space between water and earth
as indelible as if it were paint
the colour of a wave's shadow
with a hint of sandy-hue.

Farther back, far beyond my reach,
horizon meets sky in a blur
after turquoise meets deeper blue
before slipping into dove-grey
and lightening into silvery clouds,
another complex edge
where one begins and another ends.

Like you and me after the storm,
our footprints trailing us and puddling up
creating a line that will certainly disappear
as if it never was – when the light changes,
when the waves reach closer,
when time shatters this allusion too,
and lines and space and realities they separate
merge, becoming something new.

Loss Suite

Northern Cree beat drums
Guiding soul to spirit world
My heart holds you tight

I hold your strong hand
Through days, and dark, darkest night
You journey alone

Sharp talons and beak
Pierce my flesh shredding me
Grief, bird of prey, strikes

Dark descends early
Single plate on pine table
Absence tangible

Relentless grey rain
Lamps shed pools of light
Against night's abyss

Hands become brittle
Mercury pummels day
Snow clouds stack in north

Around the table
Widows with wine sit
Voices push back dark

Wind-whipped trees stand grey
Sky-dappled clouds above
Hawk rises and dives

Abandon

Shadows web across pond
join reflections of trunks
on still dark water

lost as I am in the tangle below
the abyss beckons
assures silence deep and lasting

once the pond was a fecund place
with frogs and other promises
entangled myths and lesser stories

with nightfall edges blur
merge into a well of longing
forsaken paradise falls

Falling Through Time

These are the days that narrow
at their edges, where cool arctic air
wings southward like geese
cutting a wedge through time,
chilling to the bone.

Days growing shorter follow me
into the circle garden
where I walk the ritual path,
pausing at each compass point,
realizing life's journey, like the year's,
is three-quarters full,
a harvest moon of another kind.

And so I button the flannel shirt
over my turtle neck sweater
pull on heavy gloves
and attack the final weeding,
working around the hosta,
dead-heading the black-eyed-Susan,
brushing sweetgrass through my palms.

After summer's warmth, the longest days
fall into autumn, burn like leaves
with memories of children's laughter
and grown-up dreams
before death brings
chilling dusk.

Surreal Days

Your friend drives by
in a bright yellow dump truck

I stand by a fire
dried grass, weeds, brush, and other debris
the accumulation of last year
It is quiet here in the yard
I listen to damp stems sizzle
a robin rustle grass on the hillock
a train rumbles along the track
smoke swirls around my head
I take it all in
seem to be present

I hear his horn and see his arm move
mine rises automatically in return
while my seams come undone

Winter Solstice

My heart lies heavy
buried in my chest
dense and cold as fieldstone
in late December
and if I were to stumble and
fall into the pond I'd sink
and sink and sink.

Tomorrow

This morning cloud
covers dawn
hides the sun
rain weeps
on the circle of machinery
set out for auction
in the yard by the barn.

I cradle strong black coffee
stand by the window
where rivulets stream
know that tomorrow
the auctioneer's voice
will ring out
across the farm.

The yeasty smell of rising bread
fills the kitchen
once more I will knead
shape it into loaves
to satisfy the body's need.

Nine Months

A bloody gash lies
along the horizon.
In dim pre-dawn light
I summon the circle of machinery
our dreams set out for auction.

Nine months ago
you lay in a hospital bed
and my heart was full of hope.

Now I sleepwalk through seasons
as holidays come 'round and
every letting go exposes cruel surprises.

There is a depth of pain unfelt 'til now
stirring a war within.
My soul struggles to join you
while my body breathes on.

Out in the yard shadows pale
outlines of tillage, forage
and harvest equipment solidifying.
Birds sing dawn into day.

Yesterday

rain falls in sympathy
through dawn's grey light
to drizzle down upon us
and the wagon being loaded
with power saws, wrenches
and such, while the tractor
carts the last few things
to the machinery already circled
like covered wagons of old
in the farmyard

fast following Auctioneer's arrival
pick-up trucks begin to line
both edges of the highway
and mostly men gather in groups
scatter around machines
and the wagon of "smalls"
meanwhile I escape inside our house
to privacy and mugs of coffee
but find that I cannot distract myself
and peer outside

young Jordan stands beside the auctioneer
holding trays of wrenches, screw drivers,
followed by drills and other power tools
while hands reach up to take each prize
later the list of sales will be shared with me
for now I stand hypnotized
and watch the hands raise up as
Jordan and Auctioneer move steadily
around the wagon being emptied
of the useful things you held

inside I make a fire
warding off a chill
the woodstove cannot touch
and hold our daughter's hand
a comfort as the day unfolds
and in the end
the drizzle stops
as pick-ups back to each machine
to carry them off
to other farms
other dreams

Kneading

Making bread is simple
flour, salt, honey, oil, milk and yeast
plus dried fruit and cinnamon
to toast for breakfast
or sometimes a medley of grains
to eat with robust country soup
at other times, spices
oregano and basil to perfume kitchen
and to complement risotto and veal Parmigiana

Kneading is prescribed
fold the dough toward you
push it away with the heal of your hand
turn slightly and repeat
repetition leads to meditation

Kneaded it is set aside to rise
herein is the surprise
when it has risen to twice its size
punch it down
pinch or cut in half
shape and let it rise
this time hidden in pans beneath a cloth
when almost twice its size (again)
slide into a hot oven
soon perfume scents the air
and bread satisfies our hunger

Needing is like this

Other

The face in the mirror stares
seeks what has disappeared
does not recognize eyes as hollow as pits
peaked cheeks deeply lined

she moves outside her body
bodes badly for a future
flowing like a stagnant stream
still dark abyss

entrenched in a dreamland of memory
mines love from tunnels of yesterday
yearning for embrace
empty arms rise and fall away

she drifts into the background
blackly fading into silent
stillness to roam
randomly through years undone

Gathering Lilacs

With secateurs in hand
I walk to the lilacs
reach up
and snip a cluster

cradle deep purple blooms
in the crook of my arm
add pink-edged-white
and soft mauve

breathing deeply
I inhale the blossoms' scent
see your smile
as you walk through our door

last spring
eagerness led you
to snip an early bouquet
tight blooms on our table

today tears water
clusters I place in a pitcher
blur sight
while perfume stirs memory

NORTH

*In a dream
the hooded hawk is sometimes
death; everything stops at the moment
of unmasking.*
                                — Anne Michaels

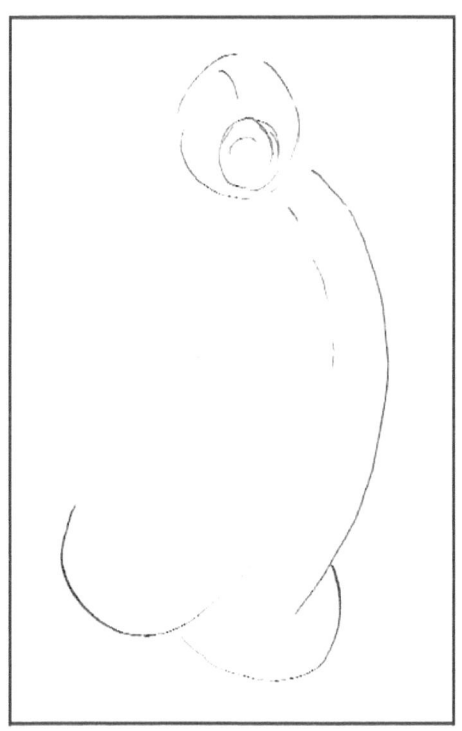

After Dark

The book lies open
on my lap
and I wait
      wait
for headlights to turn
into the drive.
I wait
      and remember that
my father
      just once
didn't turn.

Over and over
I imagine
what must have been
      what knots tangled
within my mother.

Always the voice
calm   controlled
even these years later
I feel
      the phone
slowly slowly
dropping into its cradle
feel stillness circling.
Through the quiet
I moved
      toward
the plane.

Tonight
I watch and listen
again   in fear
but the phone is for
our daughter.

That time was different
and when the plane touched
down   and the car turned

into the drive it held me
not him.   And the house
was full of neighbours.

Now waiting always grows
confused.   Time   time
moves slowly.
I would like to smash
the clock   whose hands
refuse to move
would like to watch the pieces
scatter across the floor.

The book lies open
on my lap.

Touchstone

I need a touchstone
to worry between my fingers
in the dark
and memories waken to sounds
chaining past to present
innocent things like footsteps on stairs
or images lingering like mirage
his hand on her shoulder
her eyes wide with lost innocence
an owl perches on the clothesline
barely more than a shadow
waves slap the shore rhythmically
my hands writhe in my lap
like saplings in spring wind
with nothing to grasp

Sandcastles No Longer Occupy My Hands

Once I tried
to paddle an inner tube
across the Detroit River
                              down
where it empties
into Lake Erie.

I was seven then
in pigtails with purple ribbons
    wet
        with lapping
        waves.

Still
I am carried by currents
floating
    again
my hands dipping
into indigo waters.

SEEING

She cannot
shut her eyes
when visions
cast a crow's
shadow
on sunlit snow,
but follows
through a landscape
of blue and purple
drifts that undulate
beneath tall
bare trees.
She pushes
through snow
that hides chasms
beneath its pure façade,
for searches
once begun
like cycles
must complete their course.

The literature books
tell us
that poets
are prime candidates
for suicide.

Spiritland

Shaggy grey she blends into shadows
cast by shrubs along the railroad
and I do not see her at first
only later when her yellow eyes
look hard into me.

Known by many names
like the people of my grandmother
lupus, wolf, *la loba* lives in flesh and legend.
Seldom stepping from the shadows
she lives in the woods of our dreams.

Wild life in wild spiritland
with her family pack she roams.
Instinctively predator and protector
she hunts to still the hunger
of ravenous pups and hollow self.

By day she stalks her prey
sometimes darting, sometimes surprising
in ambush; she plays her part
panicking white-tailed deer
or cow with calf at side.

By dusk she plays near cavern
doors with pups and mate and pack
mimicking the actual hunt
lesson and solace simultaneous
devotion without words.

With the rising of the moon
they lift their wild howls
to the sky
until only one remains.

But it is dawn and here we stand
sisters of a kind whose names we need not speak.
How long we pause I do not know
before we lower gaze,
turn and
return
to separate realities.

Sea Song

Through the tunnel
of the night
his drumming hooves
thrust toward
the sea wind's
      promises
        white on white
          toward the shore.

The biting wind
against my cheek
mixes sea with sea
and when the ocean
touches my face
    I feel
the whiskers grow
    I feel
my body
sleek and smooth
pulled far
into the deep
and through the furrows
of my wake
I lead the hunters
to their dream.

A woman   I
return to shore
to gather from the
hunters' knives.
In my hand
the bones take shape
and silent dreams

take flight.
On my dress
the secrets speak
in circles and in bone.
On his head
the antlers rise
a tree into the sky
and in its branches
spirits ride
singing of the sea.

Amulet Woman

The amulet woman weaves
charmed stories
charged with taut energy,
dreams, and memories.

Days along shores:
lapping water, sun-warmed bodies,
shells pocketed with river-tumbled stones
smooth-edged from their journey
into the freshwater lake.

She smells August's fullness
even as snow falls beyond her window,
tastes wind blowing up a summer storm
while caressing silver wire into a shimmering arc
around shell and stone
around moon and star.

Reading Gwendolyn MacEwan

Reading Gwendolyn MacEwan
I see the beauty of despair
– or am I just projecting this –
mirroring colours and her beads.

I grasp the polished stone between
thumb and finger, hold it tight
wrap a filament of wire
forming a twisted cage, a spider's web
to encapsulate the ancient rock
created out of fire and chaos
which circles back to Gwen
her pyre, and ashes
madness and circuses.
Reading Hiroshima I feel the guilt
and touch the garnet born in warring Afghanistan
hold it to the light to glimpse its fire
shimmering deep within.

Earth was vulgar in her birthing
grinding and groaning and spewing
torrid rivers of lava
then kneading all back into herself.
At least four times she then lay covered
in icy glaciers weighted.
Fire and ice reborn in garnet
metamorphic stone from Pluto's underworld
fiery myth caged to be worn
near my heart as Gwen
wore her beads.

May Day

She spent her days in graveyards
searching for bones
etched names
for sources.
She walked
among worn weathered
tombstones   her feet
snared by long grasses
her rhythm caught by
the river lapping against
traced ridges and crevices
of markers   and trees
right down to their roots.
She found the graves of
all her grandmothers but
could not catch their secrets
in her cupped ear.
She found fear
in the damp rich soil
in the irony of its fertility.

Landscape

Precambrian rock reaches
above earth's soil,
and down into the depths below
where granite sleeps
perhaps dreaming of volcanic
thrusts and oceanic roar
of raucous birthing sounds lost
some six hundred million years ago.

These old, old rocks
travel through time
telling stories of stars falling,
of solstices coming and going,
of warping and melting,
of burials under water and ice,
of rising like mountains
and being worn down
by wind, and sand, and unimaginable storms.

As they settled, rivers formed
and flowed, lakes too, and over time
longer than Rip Van Winkle's sleep
plains formed as the waters evaporated.
As if etched by an artist's hand
patterns took shape. Four times
snow and ice built into enormous glaciers,
advanced southward like the snout
of a frozen beast devouring plants and animals,
only to retreat northward in time,
gouging its mighty paws in a death grasp,
grinding rocks and pulling clay and rubble,
leaving behind the landscape my heart knows:
humped drumlins, and eskers of shale,
and erratic boulders plunked down
in otherwise flat farmers' fields.

My fingers caress a small stone
tossed up on the beach south of my home,
a perfect pelecypod lies embedded within,
its ridges worn smooth from the tossing
and turning of violent storms.
The pond in my garden mimics this land:
a jumble of rock waterfall,
pebbles form walkways, pink granite for sitting,
plants growing in the soil in between.

Over this landscape my ancestors trod
moving westward and southward,
but I've circled back transplanting myself
to a homeland recognized deep in my dreams,
a homeland of rocks and star-studded skies,
fulfilling a quest stretching back to my birth.
And the chalice, it seems, are these rocks
that tell stories of soulful beginnings,
of trauma, and beauty, and magic achieved.

ABOVE & BELOW

Hope is the thing with feathers
that perches in the soul
and sings the tune without the words
and never stops at all.
— Emily Dickinson

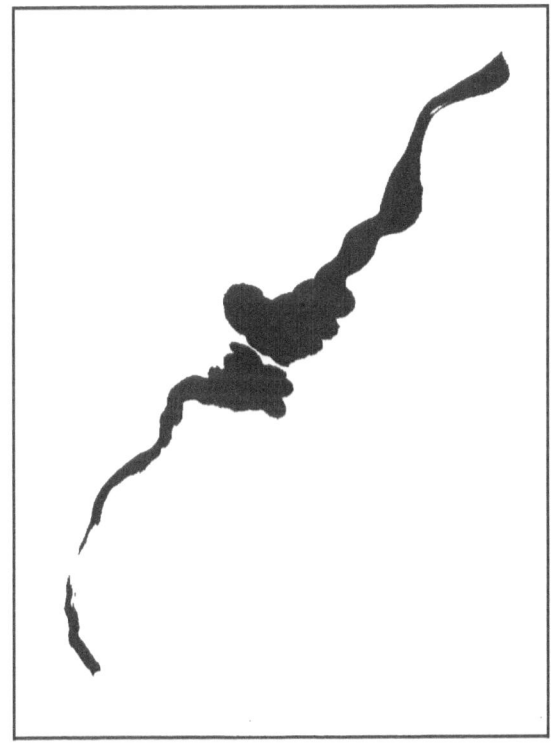

Migration

He watched fear
enter her eyes
as she bellied
through the prairie grasses.
He imagined
    the pressure
    against
her fleshy triangle as
the grasses pushed
between her legs.
Snaking forward, she,
initiation offering,
would clamp him
in her hairy, circular
    trap
    and devour
his hunger until the
fear leaped into
    his eyes.
Slowly he watched the
seeds sown in her belly
    swell.
His ear upon her naval
    listening
to drums and gurgling
    streams
to thundering hoof beats and
    rustling grasses.
From the fissure sprung
the red waters
as the migrating herds
    returned.

Mythic Alchemy

Rain slips between cloud and earth, silently.
Between hoof beats of thunder
and jagged slivers of light, it falls.
The heart in my chest quivers, remembering.
Is that a voice, whispering?
Do you hear it too?
We are all one.

Rain slips between cloud and earth, silently
Making mud from parched clay,
carrying promises and life.
The heart in my chest quivers.
Do you feel it too?
Our bodies remember that time before time
when the earth and time circled together.

It was a time before the circle was snipped.
It was a time before time stretched into a line –
from there to here and from here to beyond.
It was a time when the earth roiled
This time before time, when time was a circle of
ecstasy, like lovemaking and birthing.

Rain slips between cloud and earth, silently.
Do you feel the earth open?
Do you feel the rain seep deep inside her?
Do you feel her quiver?
Do you feel her thirst satisfied?
Do you feel her sigh – we are one?

Long ago.
Long, long ago.
Even before ONCE UPON A TIME
there was another time, an older time,
and in that time before time
earth quivered. She quivers still. Do you feel her?

In that time
sound thundered more raucous than hoof beats,
light splintered the dark so completely
no shadow was seen (had there been anyone to see it)
and ancient alchemy began its magical
shift from energy into matter.

At that time
The curious woman peered down
From the hole of the uprooted tree
From the land in the sky far above.
And she fell, making way
For mystery, for spirit.

In the beginning
earth's crust formed and split and formed again.
Scientists say it's a coming together
thickening, splitting, drifting apart,
coming together again
over eons.

And slowly, slowly Sky Woman fell
And in the myth the otter, the loon
And other diving creatures
Clawed grains from primal depths, lifting them up
Up out of the blue water, placing them
Upon the turtle's back.

Some basic elements – hydrogen, oxygen, nitrogen –
were performing a kind of magic
in time's first cauldron:
molten rock pushing up, liquid and gaseous
exploding on the surface in flowing lava
cooling quickly into fine-grained igneous rock.

Sky Woman grew larger and larger
In the eyes of the diving creatures
And the swans flew up
Spreading their wings
Easing her fall, setting her gently
Upon turtle's expanding back.

Below (trapped miles deep)
molten rock cools more slowly
and the ten times ten elements combine
in multitudinous ways, creating course-grained minerals
that in turn combine to form
plutonic rock – quartz and feldspar.

Now, Sky Woman was pregnant with life
In time, giving birth to a daughter,
Who in turn gave birth to twin sons,
Fathered by the West Wind.
But these brothers lost balance,
One quested for light, the other for dark.

Slowly, more slowly than you and I can imagine
the water became oceans and muddy rivers,
the fine-grained lava-rock became soil,
and earth became green.
Below the green earth; below the blue water
the burden of all bears down
heavy, heavier than weight,
and deep within, rock transforms.

Dark blood fell, becoming flint, becoming night.
Light built his lodge in the east,
Each dawn to ritually rise, to arc over earth
Daily chasing his brother Night from the sky.
Do you feel life stir, feel wonder
Quiver in your heart?

You know, don't you, that the jagged slivers of light
still pulse like hoof beats in the earth?
This primal urge echoes around time.
This primal urge echoes through time.
Do you hear it in thunder, see it in lightening?
Do you feel it in the rain?

Star Shower

After mid-August midnight
a near-full moon
keeps shadows at bay
on the weathered porch
and I wrap a flannel quilt
around my pale nightgown
to lay upon the old awning-swing
staring into the stars.

Surrounded by night sounds
frogs croaking down by the pond
eerie creaking in the woods
my eyes search out galaxies
as the universe opens above
to a realm blind to my daytime eyes.

Radiating from the north
these falling stars slice night above
with golden fire, arcing mysteries
outside of time, and while the early church
called them a martyr's tears
and scientists profess other theories,
I lay upon my cushion dreaming
a son's quest, dreaming a mother's rescue.

Ordinance

Birdsongs coax pearled
light across the sky and
iced mist rises to
meet the fireball's
searing renascence.
As the veil lifts
grandmother moon slips
behind a mountain ridge.
She walks
        frigid cloud piercing
        her flesh
walks
        in ritual parting
        sky and water captured in
        the fetish hanging from her neck.
And in her cave she
makes her triste
and waits.

Gifts

Eagerly I quest toward the well,
innocent of fear as if venturing into a garden
instead of a circular clearing
bounded by tall trees – cedars and pines
closing in around me as I walk.
Every footfall settles into needles
cushioning the earth,
prickling my soles,
until finally I stand before stones
ringing the dark bottomless cavern,
stones carefully stacked
one upon another
tightly wedged into wall.
I ponder the journey about to be made
down into the depths,
reminding myself of the gifts of poems
and other treasures retrieved from
fertile waters within.

On the Other Side of Sunrise

On the other side of sunrise
dark descends
a burka falling over earth

Light Quest

Shaman soul
travel with the light
across thresholds of fire and ice,
quest deep within and far beyond,
hold close the herbs and seeds of life
and chant and dance inside the ring
and in your fasting seek and seek some more
until the vision settles fully into you.

Shut your eyes and see with inner sight:
beyond the body's circle
spreads a prairie's breadth.
Endless vision encircles the world and, in your palm,
three sister seeds with points of light radiating out.
A shaman's journey has begun to warp and slip earth
As you breathe in sweetgrass and grey-green sage.

You ride light's jagged edge
sharp as a triangle of flint or hunter's knife
and reach the birthplace of *Otsistannrawan*
where souls refresh before rebirth
shimmering in the hue of icy cold
and slowly slide her dancing light
down, down into the cauldron fires of earth.

Now in your palm a snip of *esdragon*
whose roots entangle, snakes of old
curving up your wrists in druidic memory
and far beyond the ring of oaken leaves
rustling whispers to the silver moon
swing slowly in an arc above, remembering
all the old ones and their ritual celebrations.

Follow the light glowing deep
within earth's birthing belly
where lava-rivers run like living blood
pulsing to a heartbeat you cannot hear
over thundering rumble of clashing stones,
melting and merging, reforming and recreating,
where at the centre the dragon snores.

Her sharp-clawed leg stretches, both animal and bird.
Lizard scales protect her cold reptilian heart
and it is you she wants, you she reaches for.
Coward soul leap up and mount the beast
rise on her wings of fire
but, before you go, retrieve what's vital
here lying at the heart of life, and soar.

Dragon Lair

Once we knew dragons nested
where island mountains rise
between thundering seas and obscuring clouds.
Then maps forewarned danger
beyond what eyes had seen and bodies known.
Ancient rituals and journeys taken beyond fear
into life and death and life again
lay almost lost except in dark crevices
deep within mind's labyrinth and body's bones.

We flee threats, both shadow and temporal,
fail to face imagined slithering shapes
or those made real through grief or simple sadness.
But like Bluebeard's cellar where bones stack up
a tiny key lays still in a pocket
until one day a door can no longer be ignored.
Once opened illusions escape along with truer stories
we tell ourselves, stories that veil dragons
hoarding secret maps to the soul.

What did the ancients know that we have lost?
What wisdom wrapped itself inside ceremonies
of grief and celebration and the shaman's art?
Why hidden does the trauma multiply
like weedy seeds carried on the wind to fertile soil
whether earthy or within the mind?
And why (oh why) have we turned to flight
instead of facing all of life?

The mind plays tricks
we think we know
we think we understand
our selves and others
but like a magician's slight of hand
we miss the moment that escapes
into the nether land behind time's curtain
becoming memory lost in pain transformed.

But slow remembering sleep
winds a twisted passage to the soul
through burnished bones and hoards of jewels
the secret, shiny things that dragons stash.
At first they show themselves masked in dreams
and magical images or through sharp splinters of words
like shattered glass that tears away the scaly veil
until we see the spirit light glow
and dragon tongues of flame rise up.

Hitchhiker

From the highway's
edge, his thumb
begged trimmer men.
His rumpled clothes
and matted beard
bounced back from
polished paint.
He saw a stare
distorted in the
blur.   And in
the chrome
he saw a collar,
starched and white,
decrying men
who did not work.
Grandfather's stories
of hobos jumping trains
and pleading for the
farmers' milk had
come to life.
But in the shadow
that he cast
I saw myself
and sped away
like others
who had left
him walking
with their fear.

City Hunter

I watched the jazz man
reach through his horn
felt his mellow
breath caress my ears.
His dancing fingers
pushed the air
        around the
room
        rippling waves
of smoke
        broke against
my flesh
        the current
pulling toward his
plunging
        centre.

He soared and
                fell
catching his prey
in the quiet
                echo
of his rhythm.

After the Accident

Hold each other tight
as you review every memory
turning them gently like fragile Christmas bulbs.
Say his name and tell his stories.
Hold him in your heart as you once held him in your arms.
Celebrate the day that you can set his spirit free.
As once he quested from your womb,
now he's embarked upon another kind of birthing
to do the things that angels do.

Friendship

Our voices spin
words through cool evening
weaving a tapestry of stories.

Night's curtain falls
while we clear the table
carry cups of spicy chai
to woodstove warmth
and curl into chairs.

Fragments of biography
dark and light, lie side-by-side
coloured threads
creating another, our
two tales merge.

We prepare to step alone
into the dark, starless void
guided by the map of words we carry.

Acknowledgements:

Thanks to the editors of the anthologies and literary journals where versions of some of my poems were first published (some under the name Deneau):
- *Agua Terra* (Earth)
- *Close to Quitting Time: An Anthology Depicting the Various Facets of Work* (Kneading)
- *Descant xxxii-xxxiii* (City Hunter, Hitchhiker)
- *Grandmothers' Necklace* (Round, Strawberry Season)
- *Northward Journal #20* (Avatar, Migration)
- *The Fiddlehead #130* (Gardening)
- *The Wisdom of Old Souls* (Across Generations, Gatherers, Identity)

A special thanks goes to R.D. Roy who edited this collection. His insight and skill has strengthened A Breeze You Whisper, and I am grateful.

I am also indebted to my family and the many supportive friends who listened and provided feedback as the poems were in progress. Among them: Marlene Phillips, Linda Sheppard, Evelyn Lahaut, and Margaret Appleby. Three more, who stand above the crowd, are Chris Andrews (who left to sail the world), Pat Calder (who stepped into the gap), and Judith Versavel who sees things through an artist's eye.

Finally, I am thankful for knowing Jim who inspired the love poems and whose death is teaching loss and more.

Notes:

The quote in "Rehearsal" is from *Shamanism: Archaic Techniques of Ecstasy* by Mircea Eliade.

The Kiowa poet noted in "Identity" is N. Scott Momaday (from the Forward to *Keepers of the Earth*).

Otsistannrawan, in "Light Quest," is Huron for "it is dancing fire." I wish to thank John Steckley for responding to my plea.

Section Quotes:

– Liu Xiaobo, "Daybreak," PEN *America 11: Make Believe*
– Jane Hirshfield, "Pyracantha and Plum," *After*
– Lorna Crozier, "Packing for the Future: Instructions," *Before the First Word*
– Carolyn Smart, "November: Frontenac County," *The Way to Come Home*
– Anne Michaels, "The Hooded Hawk," *Skin Divers*
– Emily Dickinson, "Hope," *Poems*

Also by Kathryn MacDonald from Hidden Brook Press
www.HiddenBrookPress.com

Calla & Édourd
ISBN 978-1-897475-39-3

Drawing their sustenance from past generations, Calla and Édourd's love endures when traumatic loss gives way to fragmentation of memory, and past, present and future merge into one. MacDonald creates word paintings of nature and domestic life that linger after the last word is read. This is a beautiful story.

Evelyn Bowering, Family Therapist,
Dept of Family Medicine, Queen's University

This novella, set in Eastern Ontario, bubbles with the details of everyday life. The cycle of the seasons is reflected in the lives of the central characters. It is a hymn/lament for that which is passing and that which is past.

Alistair MacLeod,
bestselling author of short stories collected in
Island: The Collected Stories
and the award-winning novel, No Great Mischief.

www.ingramcontent.com/pod-product-compliance
Lightning Source LLC
Chambersburg PA
CBHW021112080526
44587CB00010B/489